This book is to be returned on or before
the last date stamped below.

LEARNING FOR LIFE

What do we think about

Death?

Karen Bryant-Mole

WAYLAND

Titles in the series

What do we think about

Alcohol	**Disability**
Bullying	**Drugs**
Death	**Family Break-Up**

 See page 31 for ways in which you can use this book to encourage literacy skills.

Editors: Carron Brown and Kim Protheroe
Consultant: John Bennett, a Health Education Coordinator
Cover designer: Jan Sterling
Designer: Jean Wheeler
Photo stylist: Gina Brown
Production controller: Carol Titchener

First published in 1998 by Wayland Publishers Limited,
61 Western Road, Hove, East Sussex BN3 1JD

British Library Cataloguing in Publication Data
Bryant-Mole, Karen
What do we think about death?
1. Death – Juvenile literature.
2. Bereavement – Juvenile
I. Title II. Death
306.9

ISBN 0 7502 2208 5

find Wayland on the Internet at http://www.wayland.co.uk

Picture acknowledgements
The publishers would like to thank the following for allowing their pictures to be produced in this book: Martyn F. Chillmaid *cover, title page, contents page*, 19, 22, 23, 24, 25, 26; Bruce Coleman Ltd/Werner Layer 5 (top), /Mr J. Brackenburg 5 (bottom), /Kim Taylor 6,/Simon Lancaster 7/Jane Burton 8, 9 (both), /Hans Reinhard 14; Eye Ubiquitous/Skjold 18; Getty Images'/Nicole Katano 4, /Lori Adamski Peek 10, /Don Smetzer 11, /Andrew Sacks 13, /Julian Calder 15, /Joe Cornish 16, /Jon Riley 20, /Peter Correz 21, /Peter Cade 27 (top); The Hutchison Library 17 (bottom); Impact/Norman Lomax 17 (top), /Bruce Stephens 27 (bottom); Wayland Publishers Ltd 12.

Printed and bound by Eurografica S.p.A. in Vincenza, Italy

Contents

I'm alive

To understand what being dead means, we first of all have to understand what being alive means.

This giraffe is alive.
So is this butterfly.

You are alive, too. Like
the butterfly and the giraffe, you
can breathe, eat, move and grow.

Dying

When people or animals die, the life goes out of their bodies. This bird has died because of the cold weather. The bird is dead. Its body is still there, but it has no life.

When someone, or something, dies you could think of their body as being rather like an empty house where someone used to live.

Lives

All living things have a life that follows a pattern.

These puppies have just been born. They are right at the beginning of their lives.

Over the next
few months
they will grow
bigger and
stronger.

By the time they are a year old they will
be fully grown dogs. They will be able to
have puppies of their own.

Growing old

A fully grown living thing is known as an adult.

Young adults usually have bodies that are fit and healthy. They can run fast and have lots of energy.

As adults get older, they start to slow down and their bodies begin to wear out.

Death

Death comes at the end of every life.
We are born, we live our lives and
then we die.

People die when something happens to
their body that stops it working properly.

It may have been damaged in an accident. It may have been damaged through illness or disease. It may just be worn out through old age.

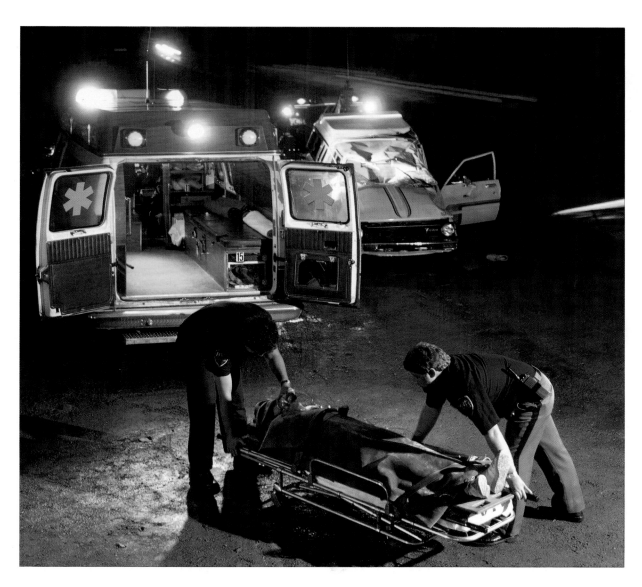

Long lives, short lives

Different living things live for different lengths of time. This hamster will probably live for about two or three years.

People are usually expected to live for about 75 years. Some people live to over 100 years old.

Just as some people live for longer, so some people have much shorter lives.

People who are very seriously ill or who have been in a bad accident can die, no matter what their age is.

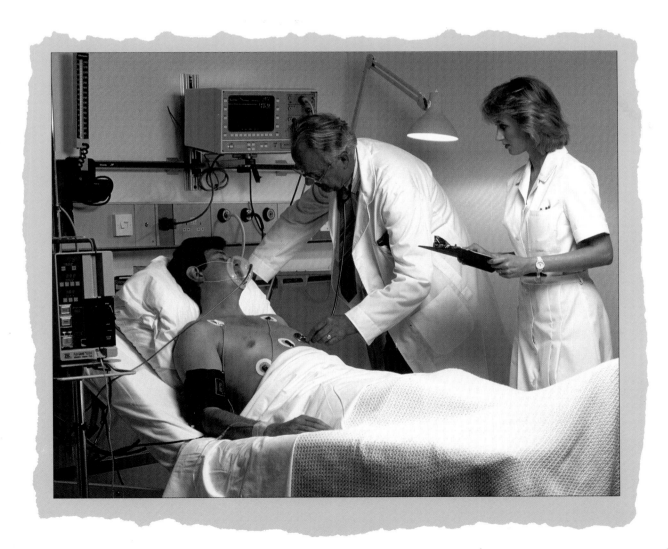

Funerals

After someone has died, there is usually a funeral. A funeral is a special ceremony. It is often held in a religious building, such as a church or a mosque.

A funeral is a chance for all the people who cared about the person who has died to come together. It is a way of saying goodbye to the person who has died.

Feeling sad

When someone dies, people who knew that person often feel sad.

People often feel sad when a pet dies, too. Lucy cried and cried when her cat died.

Feeling sad is a good thing. It shows that you really loved and cared for the person or pet who died.

Missing someone

If someone we care about goes away and we know we may not see them again, we feel sad and miss them.

If someone or something that you care about dies, you know you will not see them again and will probably miss them even more.

You might particularly miss them at special times when you used to be together.

Amy used to walk her dog in the park. After her dog died, she missed him very much whenever she went there without him.

Feeling angry

People sometimes feel cross or angry
when someone, or something, dies.

They might feel angry because they don't
think it is fair that the person they loved
has died.

Sam felt cross with himself for not telling his granny how much he loved her.

But Sam's granny probably understood that he loved her, even though he might not have said so.

Helping

It can be difficult to understand what it must feel like when someone you love dies.

Leila's friend Jack was very upset when his grandfather died. He felt sad and lonely.

Leila tried to be especially kind and thoughtful. It helped Jack to know that he had a good friend like Leila.

Remembering

It can take a long time to get over the death of someone or something you love.

Getting over a death doesn't mean forgetting. It just means that you start to feel less upset.

Instead, you
may be able
to remember
all the good
times you
had together.

Notes for parents and teachers

This book can be used in two ways. It can serve as an introduction to the sensitive topic of death. It can also be used to help and support children who have recently experienced personal bereavement. The approach is deliberately secular, allowing you, as parents and teachers, to introduce any spiritual aspects you may wish, according to your own religious beliefs. The book explains the biological process of life and death, encouraging children to understand death as part of a natural cycle. It also deals with responses to death.

Children vary enormously in their reaction to death. Often the loss of a loved family pet will have a more profound effect than the death of a grandparent or other family member who was not such a regular feature of the child's life. Not only will the response be dependent on the child's relationship with the person or, perhaps, pet who has died, but on the child's age and character, too. Young children, in particular, live in a very self-centred world and if the death has no

immediate effect on their everyday lives, they may show little emotion. Parents sometimes feel hurt by this reaction, fearing that their child is uncaring or unfeeling. But emotions cannot and should not be forced on people. In some ways perhaps it is better to be grateful that your child is not having to experience the grief that others around him or her may be feeling.

Other children may react to death with great distress. Sometimes this distress is displayed obviously, through tears and sadness, but sometimes it may be displayed as naughtiness, anger or even a withdrawing into oneself. As adults, one of the most important things you can do for bereaved children is simply to be there for them. Talking is an important part of the grieving process. Let the child know that you are there when, and if, he or she wants to talk.

Glossary

Adult A fully grown person or animal.

Ceremony A set of words and actions that are said and performed the same way each time, to mark an important event.

Church A building where people who follow the Christian religion go.

Disease An illness that can be passed on from one person to another.

Energy The strength to do things.

Fit In a healthy condition.

Funeral A special ceremony, held when someone dies.

Mosque A building where people who follow the Muslim religion go.

Pattern Something that happens in the same way over and over again.

Further information

Books to read

Death and Dying by Pete Sanders (Watts/Gloucester Press, 1995)

Grandma's Bill by Martin Waddel, illustrated by Jane Johnson (Macdonald Young Books, 1990)

Remembering Mum by Ginny Perkins and Leon Morris (A&C Black, 1996)

Remembering my Brother by Ginny Perkins (A&C Black, 1997)

Organizations which support people include:

Childline, 2nd Floor, Royal Mail Building, Studd Street, London N1 0QW   Tel: 0171 239 1000
Free helpline 0800 1111

Cruse Bereavement, Care Cruse House, 126 Sheen Road, Richmond, Surrey, TW9 1UR   Tel: 0181 940 4818

Use this book for teaching literacy

This book can help you in the literacy hour in the following ways:

- ✓ Children can use the book's contents page, page numbers, headings and index to locate a particular piece of information.
- ✓ They can use the glossary to reinforce their alphabetic knowledge and extend their vocabulary.
- ✓ They can compare this book with fictional stories about death to show how similar information can be presented in different ways.
- ✓ They can try rewriting some of the situations described in the form of a story.

Index